DOGS AND LOVE
Stories of Fidelity

by Ferris Robinson

TABLE OF CONTENTS

Egyptians Run Our Household

My sister compares me to the Egyptians, and not in a good way. She is not thinking of their amazing pyramids when she scoffs at the way they venerated cats and dogs above some humans. According to my sister, it was ridiculous the way these ancient people filled tiny feline mummies with riches for some fictitious animal afterlife.

My sister thinks domestic animals should be pets. Period. She agrees that my dogs should be fed properly and perhaps even petted occasionally. But that's the extent of it. Basically she thinks all dogs should be treated as if they were nothing more than ordinary canines. As if!

She scowls at my car full of wildly yelping livestock all franticly sliming my windows with saliva and steamy dog breath. There are only two of them actually, and they wrap me up like a maypole with their leashes, both animals beside themselves over the prospect of a walk.

She waits impatiently as I grimace and moan at the chaos, and mutter, "These dogs are driving me crazy!"

"Why don't you keep them outside; make them outside-dogs?" my sister asks flatly.

I look at her like she just suggested I never allow my children inside the house. Wait.....that's not a bad idea at all. Change that analogy to: I look at her like she just suggested I treat my tiny little Ruth Ann, and Bubba, the kindest-natured creature I've ever known, like common farm animals.

I can't imagine not having these dogs inside in the evenings. Ruth Ann curls up in my lap under a quilt, and Bubba rests his cow-sized head in my husband's lap and stares up at him with sheer gratitude.

At dinner, they wrestle with each other under the table while we sneak peeps at them between bites of broccoli. Ruth Ann is smaller than Bubba's entire head, but she somehow manages to force him to the floor and turn him until both his shoulders are pinned. He is oblivious to this defeat and rolls from side to side gleefully, accidentally tearing her little ragg sweater when it catches on his tooth. My son, a varsity wrestler, shakes his head in disgust and tells the big dog to man up.

After dinner, as we clear the table and scrape the plates, we marvel as Ruth Ann stands upright and takes tiny ballerina steps around the kitchen. We stop what we are doing and watch Bubba as he gazes soulfully off the deck, seemingly appreciating my garden.

My big hulking boys lie on the floor and talk baby talk to these dogs when they are supposed to be loading the dishwasher. Before I nag at them to get back to work, I find myself watching my boys the same way I watch my dogs: with delight.

We are not the only ones who get pleasure from our animals. My dogless neighbor slips over in the evenings with tidbits of leftover steak for Bubba and Ruth Ann, and brings her grandchildren to visit my dogs.

"Feel his ears," my neighbor says, stroking Bubba's soft flaps of ear. "They're like velvet." As the grandchildren properly oooh and ahhh over Bubba's silky ears, Ruth Ann pirouettes on her hind legs, snatching kisses from the smallest toddlers.

My brother, who lives in New York City and doesn't have a dog, strokes Bubba's head when he visits and says wistfully, "This is the exact dog I've always wanted." Bubba just looks at my brother knowingly.

Bubba and Ruth Ann chase each other through the house like bad children, scrunching up rugs and skidding around corners. I know this should not be amusing. I would never have let my children behave this way. But the fact that the dogs have been home alone all day with ample opportunity for chasing and only now that we are home can they not contain themselves, diffuses any irritation.

These dogs think the sun rises when we get up in the morning and sets when we sit down to rest in the evening. If we are apart from these dogs for more than half an hour, they spend at least that long groveling and greeting and not believing their good fortune that we have returned to them.

If we go from the kitchen to the living room, they follow us. If we walk out in the cold icy night, they accompany us. I suppose if we walked through the gates of Hell, these two dogs would be right by our sides.

So I get those Egyptians. I don't think they were ridiculous at all.

My Dog Is A Slut

I know that wanton behavior is not unusual in animals. Since the beginning of time, man's best friend has, well, put his best friend on the back burner for any little four-legged tart in heat.

What is unusual is how my husband, the father of three sons, has handled our little female dog's recent behavior.

One large male dog has been posted at our door since Ruth Ann returned home from her female surgery. Apparently there is some remnant of an intensely attractive femaleness that has kept this dog's interest piqued. That is a euphemism; he has foregone meals and stood in the freezing rain on the off-chance I decide to throw my little daschund mix at his mercy. This dog does not have an interest; he has a full blown addiction.

The first Sunday night after Ruth Ann was spayed, I sprawled out on the couch in front of the first fire of the season. My youngest son was piled up in my lap, balancing cookies and milk, as I feigned interest in professional football. Not my first choice, but I know better than to suggest we watch anything but a football game during football season. I was vaguely aware of my husband jumping up and down, something that goes along with watching football for him. But he got my full attention when he began to stomp in and out of the back door, not even within earshot of the TV.

"Would you look at her? Get up off that couch and look at her!" he bellowed from the other end of the house.

I rearranged the cookies, the glasses of milk and my little boy and looked out the window at Ruth Ann scampering playfully around the large dog. She jumped up on him, covering his eyes with her paws flirtatiously. Besides the male dog sniffing around her privates, there was nothing offensive going on. I told my husband if anything bad was going to occur, it would have happened already. I made it back to the TV just in time to see Tampa score.

Incensed, my husband brought Ruth Ann inside, but she was not so glad to be rescued. She stood with her paws up on the window, transfixed and panting, as the strange dog finally wandered away.

When she began to yelp and scratch frantically at the window, my husband began to rant and rave again.

"Would you look at her? What is she doing? She acts like she actually *wants* to go back outside!!!"

Now, as the mother of three boys, I am finally over not having a girl. I have come to terms with not having a daughter to take to lunch every week, to get manicures with and take shopping for pink, frilly clothes. Granted, it was an adjustment, but one I have made.

However, my husband's tirade over the dog's courtship shed new light on this issue. For the first time, I was actually thankful I did not have a daughter. My husband is a stellar father for sons. He has the perfect amounts of toughness and tenderness. He handles pierced ears and back-talk the same way he handles fevers and honors: with confidence, and in my opinion, perfectly. With boys, he knows exactly what to do. I cannot count the times I've stood back as he dealt with various learning opportunities and thought, "Now that's a mistake," as he interacted with one of my boys. And then scratched my head over the positive outcome.

Over the years, I've had hints that he would be in foreign territory with daughters. My boys and I have looked befuddled at both his tone of voice and word choice when he talks to their girl cousins. Syrup drips off his words for no reason.

As I witness my husband's frustration over our little female dog, my blood runs cold as I imagine a teenaged daughter interacting with him. Spaghetti straps? Exposed midriff? Mini skirts? A combination of all the above?

I have a feeling his reaction to the dog in heat would be mild compared to his outrage over a daughter dating.

And suddenly both the Bucs and my three boys look very good.

The Lost Mother Dog

It was clear the dog had a home of her own once, that she was used to humans. She wagged her tail enthusiastically, greeting any person she saw, but wouldn't come close to anyone.

What happened to that home is anyone's guess. But beginning in early May, just after the tornadoes came through Georgia in 2011, the white dog with the black patch over her eye regularly roamed through the college campus on the bluff of Lookout Mountain and through several nearby neighborhoods. She was friendly, but wouldn't look anyone in the eye, keeping her head down submissively. People wondered if she'd gotten lost after the storms, if her owners had been displaced. Or if someone had simply abandoned her on the highway.

Pregnant and on a mission to find a safe place to deliver her puppies, the mother dog was clearly starving.

People in the neighborhood overlooking the brow began leaving food out for the dog, and unbeknownst to them, a college student a mile down the road was doing the same thing. A woman from the neighborhood was on her own mission: she was determined to save the mother dog. She couldn't stop thinking about the poor, bewildered animal once sleeping at her master's feet, curled up in a safe spot. She tried to lure the dog close with food, but to no avail.

The animal took the food greedily, never meeting her eye, then hurried away.

No one knew where she'd gone to have her puppies; only that she'd had them. Several times a day the mother dog crawled up through the thickets covering the bluff to search for food, then crept back down. Her ribs became clearly visible under her fur, and she moved slower and slower, not wasting energy on wagging her tail anymore.

When the woman's grown son saw the desperate mother dog crawling back down the mountain with a box turtle in her mouth, he followed her down the bluff to rescue the puppies. He fought through thick blackberry bushes and dense undergrowth, watching all the while for rattlesnakes. Someone had been bitten the week before.

He came to an abrupt stop on a ledge above a sheer cliff. There was a crack in the rock leading to a cave, but it was too dangerous to climb up to the opening. He heard the puppies crying deep within the rock, but couldn't reach them. He reassured the animals he'd be back, and as he fought his way through briars, he wondered how he would ever get to the cave.

The mother dog quickly wolfed down anything left out for her, but she couldn't eat enough to sustain her treks up and down the side of the mountain to care for her puppies. The mother dog was getting weaker and weaker. Her bones were even more prominent as she trudged slowly back and forth, seeming unsure and panicked.

The puppies would soon be mobile, and the woman knew where their first tentative steps would lead them. The cave was on a sheer drop-off.

Determined to rescue the puppies, the woman's son went back down the bluff, this time with an extension ladder. But when he reached the ledge, his heart sank. There was no sound of the puppies. He strained to hear a whimper. A soft cry. Any sign of life. But the cave was dead silent.

He tried not to think of the puppies he'd never even seen. He didn't want to imagine them plummeting to their deaths as they took their first steps out into the light of day. He didn't allow the image of coyotes finding the helpless little animals. Or a rattlesnake. He walked up the steep side of the mountain with a heavy heart. And he dreaded telling his mother the bad news.

The last time anyone saw her, the white dog staggered through the neighborhood, no longer on a mission. She barely had the strength to walk, much less wag her tail. It was clear the dog could not survive much longer. Her death meant the certain death of her puppies, if they were even alive.

Distraught over the dire situation, the woman from the neighborhood stopped by the college to ask if anyone knew anything about spelunking. She hoped if someone could get inside the cave, one of the puppies might still be alive. She knew if they could get the puppies to safety, even one of them, the mother dog would follow.

When she explained the situation to a student, his face lit up and he reached for her hand.

"You've got to see this," he said, leading her to the student apartments. She saw the porch in the distance, littered with an old couch, a bike and some boxes, and wondered why he thought she'd be interested in such a mess.

She thought she saw something move, and there, on the couch, were four tiny puppies, snuggled up against their mother. One of them had a black patch over its eye.

"I woke up one morning and there was a puppy on my porch. The next morning there were two, and then three the next. That mother dog spent the whole night bringing one puppy up at a time, four nights in a row," the student said.

This mother dog had suddenly found herself in a strange place for whatever reason and all she knew to do was take care of her babies. She bore them in the safest place she could find, a cave on the side of mountain, safe from prying humans, speeding vehicles and wild animals.

She must have known she was going to die, that she couldn't survive many more hours. Somehow that mother dog knew she needed to get her puppies up from the bluff before she died, and she knew the old, mildewed couch on the porch was safer than the cave. And for some reason, she decided to trust the upright, two-legged things that were sometimes kind, and sometimes not so kind.

The mother dog looked up at the woman with dark, melted chocolate eyes, meeting her gaze finally. Slowly getting up from the couch, the dog wagged her tail, and nudged the woman's hand with her nose, greeting her like they were old friends.

Named Dot for the black spot over her eye, the dog now lives happily with the woman, and every puppy found a good home.

My Dogs Clearly Prefer Me to a Movie Star

My sister thinks I should keep my dogs outside.

"They're dogs," she says irritably when they skid on clawed toes across my foyer.

I don't tell her Tom Cruise has nothing on their *Risky Business* rendition.

"They were meant to live outdoors," she says, rolling her eyes at Ruth Ann's new red corduroy coat.

I can see how she might think Bubba and Ruth Ann are canines. They have thick fur coats year round, eight legs between them and very sharp teeth. But for the most part, that is where the similarities end.

My dogs may not speak plain English, but they don't have to. They live in a household full of eager translators.

"Bubba says he's glad we're home," my husband says as Bubba moans in ecstasy at his feet.

"Ruth Ann thinks that bacon is for her," my son interprets as Ruth Ann sits on her tiny haunches expectantly, watching me poke at the bacon sizzling in the skillet.

"Bubba appreciates my fire," my husband says pointedly to me as Bubba sits still beside the hearth, mesmerized by the flames.

We get a ridiculous amount of pleasure from these two animals. We laugh out loud when Bubba balances his sixty-pound frame on the edge of my chair and pretends he is a lap dog. We are amused when tiny Ruth Ann leaps in the air to attack Bubba's throat, like the benevolent softie is something to be feared. And we coo when Bubba sleeps with his paws clasped under his chin like an angelic child.

"He is too much of a gentleman," my son says when Bubba backs away from his food dish, offering Ruth Ann his food.

"Ruth Ann adores Bubba," I say when she curls up under the big dog's shoulder in front of the fire.

"Well, they're totally co-dependent," my husband says critically, as if we should take them to an Al-Anon meeting.

But he's right. The tiny black min pin-daschund mix must have Bubba's undivided attention at all times, and he hers.

In the evenings, the dogs are key to our relaxation. When my husband lies flat on the floor to ease his back, Bubba lies alongside him, resting his head on my husband's shoulder like an affectionate wife. Meanwhile, Ruth Ann burrows under my afghan and sleeps in my lap, snoring out loud every now and then, as any tension left over from my day dissolves. I translate for these creatures my sister thinks are mere animals; they love their evenings at home.

But the majority of what these two tell us needs no translation.

Bubba looks steadily into my eyes, unblinking and with the most tender expression I've ever seen. No one needs to interpret what he's saying in English, or any other manmade language. *You are undoubtedly the most special person on earth and I would do anything for you. I cannot believe my good fortune to belong to you.*

So I ignore my sister's disapproval of my 'inside dogs' and welcome them to the kitchen. They can't get over the fact that I am home and greet me as enthusiastically this millionth time as they did the very first time. They sniff me and kiss me and tell me I am magnificent and wonderful and beloved above all others. They clearly proclaim that any man, even Tom Cruise, would be lucky to have me.

At least that's my interpretation.

A Great Man. And His Dog

I didn't know Jack Lupton. But I do know his dog.

Mopsy is a little lap dog with long white hair and bandages on her front legs. She is old, almost fourteen, and has terrible arthritis. The day I met her, the day of Jack's funeral, I couldn't look away from her dark, heartbreaking eyes.

Mopsy huddled under her master's kitchen table, peeping up at the commotion. The Lupton children and their spouses and their children and his great-grandchildren all gathered in the kitchen, a large family preparing for a terrible day.

When the family left in the limousine, Mopsy walked slowly back to her beloved master's bedroom and sniffed at the bed. She limped over to his favorite chair, then to the window seat. She searched for him in all the places she'd found him before.

I discovered the little dog in the bathroom, sitting on a dressing chair. Mopsy found a quiet place away from the strangers watching over her house. Away from me. I petted her, whispered to her, then left her alone for a while.

When I went back to check on her later, Mopsy had moved to the closet. She was burrowed back under the hanging clothes, shivering.

I couldn't stand watching the little animal mourning her master all alone, away from her family. She let me pick her up and bring her to the den, where I sat with friends, watching over the house while the family buried their patriarch. She tolerated me, a stranger, for a few minutes. Then hobbled back to the closet.

One of Mr. Lupton's caregivers came by for a few minutes, and Mopsy crept into the kitchen on her poor crippled legs. The little dog must have heard the caregiver's familiar voice, and wondered if it was a sign. A clue as to where her master was. Mopsy sniffed at the front door, the door the woman had just come through, and looked up at me expectantly. Then the little dog traced the path the woman had walked, around the kitchen, through the laundry room. But the nurse was already gone.

I knew the funeral would be packed; Mr. Lupton was an exceptional man.

Mopsy had no idea of her master's outstanding accomplishments in the human world. She knew nothing of the Tennessee Aquarium he had instigated and funded, or the Honors Golf Course he had built or the plethora of community foundations he had established. The little dog could not comprehend that the man she nestled against morning, noon and night, had changed both the landscape and the future of a city.

Mopsy only knew that Jack Lupton, the man who held her little body against his chest and whispered to her and loved her, was her champion. And that her master, her constant companion, the man whose lap may as well have been hers, was her hero.

I imagine Mopsy soothed him toward the end. Comforted him with her unconditional love and adoration, based solely on her canine instincts.

When her master took his last breath, Mopsy let out a sharp yelp, then released a long, slow moan.

I walked fretfully around the house I was watching over, trying to comfort Mopsy. An embroidered pillow caught my eye in the living room; it was small and bright, out of place with the tasteful furnishings. I picked it up and rubbed my fingers over the letters. "God, Let Me Be The Man My Dog Thinks I Am."

I think Jack Lupton can check that one off.

16

The Forbidden Dog

I remember clearly the day my husband put his foot down. "We are NOT getting a new puppy! Over my dead body!" my husband declared when my son announced the only thing he wanted for his birthday was a dog.

And so my son and I went straight to the pound to pick out his 18th birthday present. We scanned the cages full of puppies, and found one little dog shivering in the cage, her brow furrowed with worry. When my son picked her up, she put her head down on his shoulder and gazed up at him with liquid brown eyes, making herself the easy choice.

More human than canine, Ruth was the little girl I never had, and I dressed her accordingly. She didn't have much in common with other dogs. When Bubba, our bona fide dog, roughhoused and tumbled with other dogs, Ruth stepped delicately to the side, looking up at me disapprovingly. While Bubba leapt in the lake and paddled after sticks, she stood at the edge of the water and scolded him. And when I walked her on a leash, she held it daintily in her mouth, making it clear she was quite civilized and if anyone needed to be restrained, it was me.

In the evenings, she curled up in my lap, under my afghan. And the warm little breathing ball of animal snuggling contentedly against me was like a tonic. No matter how stressed or agitated I may have been, I was limp and relaxed within minutes of her dozing in my lap.

She had a crush on my middle son the season they were the same age; she was two and a half, and he was sixteen. When he was around, she rolled over on her back with one paw in front of her face and gazed at him as coquettishly as last month's centerfold. And she was as jealous as any woman could be. This son was not allowed to pet the other dog, or even look Bubba's way.

Ruth Ann's animosity never fazed Bubba. He loved her most of all. In the morning when they came out of the laundry room where they slept, he would stare down at her with affection and delight, no matter that he usually slept on the floor while she had her choice of the two beds. I told my husband that if he could ever love me as much as Bubba loved Ruth he would go down in history, heads and tails above Wallis Simpson and the Prince of Wales.

It didn't take my husband very long to be completely won over by this tiny, ferocious, delightful little girl. "How's my precious girl?" he cooed in a ridiculous singsong voice when he came home from work. We all knew he wasn't talking to me.

When my oldest son, Ruth's original master, announced he would be taking her off to college with him, my husband drew the line once again. "Over my dead body," he declared.

This time my son backed down.

Ruth Ann gave us more pleasure than we deserved. She lightened our burdens and put joy in our hearts. And because of Ruthie, some of our darkest moments were more bearable.

We loved her. And we appreciated her. We knew how terrible this moment would be, the moment we lost her forever. We had hoped it would be when she was old, after a whole lifetime with us.

My middle son wrapped her still body up in the afghan one last time and dug her little grave in the garden as I sobbed.

Bubba lay by her grave all afternoon, desolately standing guard over her little body.

We understood his grief all too well.

Mourning

My big dog Bubba sits quietly at my feet, utterly lost. My whole family is lost, in a sense. But unlike Bubba, we understand that our little black dog, Ruth Ann, is dead. We do not look for her.

We don't dig furiously in the gigantic hole she worked on daily, hoping she is in there, maybe only resting after her vigorous digging.

We don't smell the spot in the road frantically, the last place she was fully alive. When the family station wagon pulls in the drive way, we don't run to the rear door, hoping she might jump out.

We understand her body is buried on the hill behind the garden, just outside my bedroom window. I know better than to sit in my bedroom chair to drink my coffee; I can't bear to see her grave.

My husband and I don't take a nap this weekend because Ruth Ann will not be there to stretch out across my husband's chest. It is so sad to think she will never again curl up in my lap under the afghan, her body so light it was more warmth than weight.

We scrape our choice leftovers straight into Bubba's bowl without making him perform first. We don't insist he sit or stay, something we always did after dinner with the two of them. Now, the day after we lost Ruth Ann, we clean up the kitchen quietly. We don't play music because we can't bear to remember Ruth Ann dancing to Thriller with our youngest son, her tiny black paws in his.

The morning after she died, I sit on the edge of my bathtub, trying to pull myself together. I hear something in the kitchen, and for an instant I think it's the rapid clicking of her little toenails as she rounds the corner at full speed, pleased with herself for finding me. It's not her, of course. As a human, I understand why.

It's different at our house now. It is quiet. We don't hear her quick high pitched yip early in the mornings. When we watch TV now, there is no trilling from her to be petted. When we come home, we are not greeted by a mad dog race complete with ecstatic moaning and yelping and kisses.

Now, in the mornings, I have to make Bubba get up out of his bed. I lure him with choice tidbits. When we come home from work, he barely lifts his head to greet us.

I pick up Ruth Ann's collar and fold her red corduroy coat and put them away for good. I take up her bowl and shake out her blanket before washing it. I know it is time to move on. I know in my head that the accident and the surgeries and the trauma were too much for her little body, and that it was probably a blessing that she died. But Bubba doesn't know this. He just knows that his leader is gone.

She dictated when he was allowed to eat (after she had finished) and how much. She decided when it was time to play high-speed chase through the house (when we wanted to unwind) and when it was time to work on the hole in the yard. She let him know when to get out of the lake and when to chase the squirrels, when to go outside and when to come back in. She decreed which bed was his (the small old one) and which one was off limits (the new large one).

But every single night, she slept curled up in a ball against his chest.

Three days after Ruth Ann died, Bubba finds her little torn ragg sweater stuffed in the chair cushion. He brings it to me in his mouth, shoving it against my leg like it might be a clue. He looks up at me with sorrowful eyes, searching mine for an answer.

I am lost as to how to comfort him.

My Mother's Blind Dog

Molly's life would have been different if she'd lived on a farm. Or next to decent people.

Her barking irritated one of their neighbors, but he never complained to my parents. He just threw acid in her face one afternoon, destroying her eyes. Distended and ruined, her eyes turned into something out of a horror movie, and my mother drove the dog to Knoxville for several surgeries. Finally the team of veterinarians had to remove both eyes, and stitch her eyelids together.

My first reaction was to put her to sleep; I thought life would be too miserable for a blind dog. But my mother slowly nursed the dog back to good health, patiently and carefully walking her though the house, showing her the furniture, the doors, the hallways. No piece of furniture was allowed to be moved after Molly learned where it was.

During that trauma, the bond between my parents and Molly became more than merely dog and masters. When Molly ran into a chair, as she rarely did, my parents rushed to her and comforted her more than I ever remembered being coddled for a skinned knee.

The dog was terrified of thunder and lightening and once a summer storm came up unexpectedly while my mother was away doing errands. Molly broke the clip of her leash and ran in a panic down toward the four-lane highway near their house.

We looked everywhere for her, calling neighbors, contacting stores, wringing our hands.

My mother could not stop thinking of how terrified and confused Molly must be. She did not sleep for two nights, and barely ate for two days. My mother's voice was weak, sick with worry.

We finally found her in the woods down the hill from my parents' house. A stone's throw away from my mother's bedroom window. Molly's leash had tangled in a bush, trapping her. She just sat silently in the rain, as if she was mute as well as blind.

Molly lived for nearly ten years after that. She nuzzled my mother's chin with her nose instead of making eye contact. And lay her head across my father's feet when she rested.

She was a beautiful animal, with downy chestnut hair that you just had to touch.

And then Molly got cancer and began having strokes when it reached her brain. Each week there was a new tumor that we could feel under her coat. She lost her keen sense of direction and began bumping into furniture she had always managed to avoid.

Heavy hearted, my mother cared for her dog, boiling chicken tenderloins and dicing them up for her. She cleared out the furniture in her den, making an open path for Molly.

Soon Molly began to get lost in the house and would sit bewildered in the hall, crying. She walked bent over, her head hanging down to one side, and then she couldn't walk at all.

They finally took her to Dr. Keller. My father carried the thin, limp dog that had been their constant companion for the last decade and a half. My mother made my father sit in the waiting room, protecting him from watching the actual death. My mother stood over Molly, stroking the dog's head and speaking in her gentle voice.

"It's alright, Molly, it's alright darling girl," my mother said.

Molly took her very last breath alongside my mother's face. The face the dog hadn't seen in over a decade was wet with love and grief as my mother's tears fell onto the dog's head, trickling over her eyes, and making them glisten.

Anna the Amazing

About ten years ago, just after Molly died, a black dog appeared under the deck of my parent's isolated cabin in middle Tennessee, and they just happened to be there. Mangy, starving and terrified, the animal snarled menacingly if they got too close, but this did not deter my mother. She was crouched under the deck, offering the poor creature bits of turkey, when Animal Control pulled up in the driveway. Two uniformed men jumped out of the truck with all manner of dog-catching apparatus and announced they'd gotten a report of a stray dog at this address.

"There's no stray dog here!" my mother said authoritatively as the dog growled at her. "This is my dog!"

My father just looked sheepishly at the animal control people and shrugged.

It took my parents a while to lure the feral dog into the car, and the newly-named Anna gave the vet a run for his money.

Anna was no easy pet. Devoted to my mother, she was suspicious of my father (for good reason – animal control was on his speed dial), and aggressive toward everyone else, including grandchildren. Her coat was patchy and dull, and she was literally skin and bones. She was terribly destructive, tearing up the new sprinkler system triumphantly, proud of the protection she gave my mother against the threatening, hissing monster in the garden. She riddled my mother's new car with so many long claw scratches there seems to be a unique striped pattern on the driver's door. She nibbled all the bedspreads, and the corner of the damask sofa.

Anna panics when it rains, whirling in desperation like some kind of possessed dervish, and seems to have psychotic episodes in the middle of the night, for no apparent reason.

Anna is not the ideal house pet. I tell them they need to figure this out, that she is much too destructive.

But it doesn't matter. She's my mother's dog.

When she ran through her electric fence because she was afraid of the workmen, we searched for her night and day. We looked north and south, east and west. Up the mountain. Down the mountain. Everyone we knew combed the neighborhood, calling her name.

She had seemingly vanished into thin air. After five days, I told my mother Anna had died. And I convinced myself she had. There was not a trace of her anywhere.

I took my mother to the pound to get a new dog, knowing that was the only way to heal her grief. She walked slowly through the kennels, not considering any other dog, but just looking for Anna. "I feel like she's trapped somewhere, waiting on me to rescue her," my mother said, clearly tormented.

Seventeen days after she went missing, a neighbor heard a dog faintly whimpering near his home. He couldn't tell where it was coming from, and walked up and down the street until he finally realized the dog was trapped underground. He called the police and the vet and within minutes a fire engine appeared and the crew pulled the mostly dead animal from the ground. 80% dehydrated and septic from multiple wounds that went down to her tendons, Anna was barely alive.

I rushed to animal hospital on a Sunday afternoon, just in time to watch Anna have a seizure and code on the table.

I was waiting in the hall when my mother got there. We strained our ears for sounds, any hint at what was going on, then heard a series of exclamations, and knew it was good news.

She was alive, but on a respirator. The doctor gently told my mother that Anna may have brain damage, and too poor a quality of life, but they would cross that bridge later.

Anna lay limp on the table, an empty shell of a creature. Her eyes were rolled back in her head, and the stench of necrosis from her wounds was terrible. My mother stroked the dog's head and told her what a good girl she was, until Dr. Keller finally sent her home. He checked on the dog through the night, calling the next morning to say she was still alive, but cautioned she was not out of the woods.

Monday morning she was off the ventilator, but still not moving. Dr. Keller pulled a chair up for my mother, and she spent the day rubbing Anna's head and comforting her.

"It's a miracle," someone who had been in the operating room said.

Monday afternoon, they propped Anna up and she wolfed down a can of food.

By Tuesday, Anna and my mother were 'receiving' on Dr. Keller's front porch, but there was too much stimulation for the traumatized animal and she had two seizures.

Wednesday afternoon my mother called me, ecstatic. "She pulled out her I.V. in the night!" she said.

Thursday my mother gushed that Anna was a different animal, sitting up like a sphinx and looking around. She rushed over the part about Anna being blind, and completely crippled.

I wondered how my mother was going to take care of a crazy blind dog that was apparently paralyzed, but I don't say anything.

I didn't sleep for two nights after she was found; I couldn't stop thinking about her trapped underground, hearing us calling her name. How could I not have thought to look down when we searched for her? It turns out, Anna ran and hid in a drain a few yards from my mother's house, but couldn't back out. She could only move forward. So she just crawled straight ahead, day after day after day. Squeezed so tight the hot metal scraped her fur off. Then her skin.

So yes, Anna is coming home. And we will figure out the rest of it.

The New Dog

We all pretended the new dog was for Bubba.

"He looks depressed," we said about the morose hound dog lying on the wooden floor.

"He's so lonely by himself all day," we all said, worried as Bubba barely looked up at us from his bed.

The truth was, we each knew exactly how the dog felt because we felt the same way. If something clattered onto the floor, I immediately thought of Ruth Ann's tiny claws skittering across the wooden floor. My husband sat in front of the TV in his worn fleece vest and felt a chill across his chest where she used to snuggle, zipped up snugly against him.

Our hearts were heavy.

"You need a new dog," my neighbor told me. "That's the only way your heart will heal."

I went to the Humane Society two months after our little dog, Ruth Ann, died. We'd decided to adopt a little dog from the pound because we thought it was the right thing to do; so many dogs needed homes.

I walked through the maze of dog-filled pens, and felt like putting my hands over my ears to muffle the barking. I wanted to pinch my nose to lessen the stench of hundreds of trapped dogs. Most of these poor animals yelped frantically and leapt toward the top of the cage. Some sat still and looked at me sadly, like they knew it was futile to act interested. I couldn't meet their eyes.

I searched for a certain dog, a little black dachshund-min-pin mix, knowing I wouldn't find one. I finally took three little dogs, one at a time, to the pebbled play-yard. I tried to give them a chance, get to know them a little. One fluffy black dog sat calmly in my lap, as docile as could be. One brown puppy ran around the edge of the play-yard vigorously, but didn't glance at me once. One squatty tan dog with a Chihuahua face leapt up into my lap and kissed me on the mouth before he skedaddled around the yard. A minute later he vaulted back into my lap and nuzzled my neck.

I brought two of my sons, my sister and my husband down the meet this little affectionate dog, all on separate occasions. They all approved, and I filled out the paperwork, and paid the fee. He would be a good dog, I told myself. He was friendly and enthusiastic.

Two days before the little dog was scheduled to be neutered, I had second thoughts. He was tan, not black like Ruth Ann. He was male, not female, and furry, not sleek like an otter. And he was almost twice her size. I didn't want a furry tan dog; I just wanted my little black dog back.

I decided to wait, thinking sooner or later, I would come across a perfect little black dog like Ruth Ann.

I called the Humane Society to cancel the little dog, and they told me I had to bring my receipt in for a refund. When I got there, the woman behind the desk was on the phone, so I walked back to the tan dog's cage. He saw me, and I believe he remembered me.

I think he knew I am a huge flake, and needed reassurance that he was the right dog. Or maybe he just knew he was the right dog. He didn't bark like all the other dogs, or scramble frantically in his cage. He just looked up at me pleadingly searching my soul with big bulging Chihuahua eyes. I reached through the cage to scratch his ears, and he pressed the side of his head against my hand and wagged his tail, peering up at me with one googly eye.

I told the poor, overworked woman in the office that I had changed my mind. Again. I told her I did want the little dog after all. So she had to re-enter all of my info on the computer and check over the paperwork and call the vet to reschedule his surgery. I told her not to take any more of my calls.

We all braced ourselves for the arrival of the new little dog. We knew there would be an adjustment period of barking through the night and house training accidents and chewing up things that were not meant to be chewed. But there wasn't. Victor didn't make a peep when I put him in the laundry room with Bubba for the first night. He seemed to be housetrained already, and so far the only thing he's chewed is a corn cob that I had chewed on already.

It's uncanny how much like Ruth Ann he is. He lies in wait by the lake and attacks Bubba when the big dog comes up out of the water. He snatches a pair of white socks off the floor and trots off with them victoriously. He stretches out on my husband's chest and gazes up at him.

We watch him jump up on Bubba's back like a cat. Bubba collapses on the floor and acts foolish while the little dog roughhouses. Bubba looks up at us as if to say, "I know he is a pale-coated, long-haired fluffy male, but he is just right."

I think that's how we all feel.

Puppy Training – Who's Training Who?

I am determined to house train this new puppy. I take him outside several times a day, my pocket heavy with treats. I say "Hurry up!" like my training manual suggests so that Victor will learn to relieve himself immediately upon hearing that phrase.

On a mission, I walk him down the path to my garden. So far he is in no hurry at all, despite my suggestions. Instead he sticks his nose in a clump of bee balm and sniffs. I pinch off a red fringed blossom and squeeze it in my hand, breathing in the sharp fragrance.

"Hurry up!" I coax as he meanders along the path, smelling the carmine-red spiraea and the tips of the lavender and the frothy yellow yarrow that spills over the path. Finally I give up and take a seat on the wooden bench my husband gave me a few years ago. It is the perfect accent piece for my garden, but to my knowledge, has never been used. I am glad to have a spot in the shade to wait. "Hurry up!" I say again as he wanders further down the path.

I have spent countless hours in this garden, but I am always working on a project. I weed constantly. I keep the bird feeder full and the hydrangeas watered and I spread pine straw on a regular basis. When I look at my backyard it is to see what needs replacing and what needs to be added.

This is the first time I have ever sat down and looked at my garden without criticism. I am still. Right beside me an oversized bumblebee trundles over a violet butterfly bush bloom. The bee clings, now upside down, to the conical blossom that has rolled over under the insect's weight. Undeterred, he continues his mission, frantically eating pollen with what appears to be six hands.

There is a butterfly on another bloom, methodically opening and closing his brown and orange wings. I lean in closer and peer at his busy whirl of antennae as he vigorously sips up nectar. He seems completely unaware of me.

I am still. There is another bee so close to me I could touch him, but he looks different. His tiny body is a soft mossy green and he has a fan tail. Suddenly I realize it is not a bee at all, but a baby hummingbird. His whirring wings make no noise and I wonder if the motorized hum grown hummingbirds make comes with age. I don't move as I watch him immerse most of his little torso in a single bloom of a vivid pink phlox. I listen hard to see if I can hear him. I can't.

Instead, I hear the trill of a bird from the woods, then a repetitive chirp-chirp-chirp of another, and then a frenzied twitter of what must be a flock of the same bird. I cannot see any of these birds, but know I am hearing different ones.

A goldfinch glides in for a perfect landing on my full feeder. He is bright crayon yellow and pops out against the black sunflower seeds. I drink him in.

My puppy comes barreling down the path and jumps up on my lap, joyfully licking my chin. Victor has sniffed every flower and chased every bee and noticed every single thing in the garden. I glance at my watch and realize almost half an hour has passed and I have no idea if my mission was accomplished or not. Still, I do not tell him to hurry up.

I feel the vibration of the baby hummingbird just behind my ear, but I never hear a sound. The leaves rustle and there is a late summer breeze on my face and I think what a lovely spot I have in the world. I am thankful my little dog has not learned how to 'hurry up'. I gaze out at the garden and think of all I would have missed if he had. I stroke my little dog's ear and wonder if that was his mission all along.

My World is a Dog's World

I don't know what I'm going to do about my dogs. Really. They are a workout. I am not the "pack leader", but instead a namby-pamby, semi-master who can only make them sit at one specific time, and in one specific area. The kitchen.

Immediately after dinner, they sit beside the dishwasher. They hunker down on their haunches, expectantly waiting for a bite of the chicken they saw me eating at dinner. They both look like model dogs, perfectly trained to, well, sit.

If I instruct them to sit at any other time of day, or in any other place, they act like they've never heard the command. They practically roll their eyes at each other, and ignore me, saying, 'what-ever' in dog language. I may as well have two more teenagers.

It gets worse. Bubba, my big red bone hound, has laid claim to the sofa. I made the mistake of letting him on it after our little dachshund died last spring, when Bubba looked so bereft and lost. It was supposed to be a little comfort for a night or two. Something to ease his pain a little bit.

Now, seven months later, he sprawls across the full length of the couch, growling when I try to wedge my large rear between him and the arm of the sofa.

I might even tolerate his commandeering the couch if he would stay put for more than five minutes. He doesn't. He wants out, then back in, then back out, in cycles that can be measured in single digits. He never wants to go out when I am on my feet and easily mobile, only when I am tucked in on my sliver of the sofa.

So instead of conversing over dinner or relaxing by the fire or curling up to read, my family takes turns answering the door when the dog wants in, then opening it back up when Bubba wants out. I imagine us in fast motion, an animated cartoon.

My little dog, Victor, is quieter, but definitely has issues. He is both sneaky and a thief. Infinitely nosy, he loves nothing more than rooting through bags, be it a cosmetic bag, a hand bag or a grocery bag. He rummages through my son's backpack on a regular basis, chewing up pens and old lifesavers with equal gusto. I've replaced my make up brushes twice since he joined our family and my disgusting nighttime mouthpiece once (Victor does not think it's disgusting at all). Last night he appeared with a cellophane bag of blood meat catfish bait from my son's tackle box, and I won't begin to describe the aroma.

You might wonder how he gets these things. I wondered the same thing myself when my son complained that Victor had gotten his girlfriend's cell phone for the third time. He had already been through her make-up bag and her suitcase.

We close our closet doors and put things-of-interest on high shelves and for the most part, keep our mouthpieces and catfish bait in closed drawers. But if a packed bag sits by the door for a minute before departure, or if the cell phone is set down for a second while someone gets a drink or the pocket book is left in the car while groceries are unloaded, that little Victor sees a flicker of opportunity, and pounces.

The other morning I made breakfast for my husband before he left for work, a rare treat he was looking very forward to. I set the heaped plate on the counter and walked back to the bedroom to tell him breakfast was served.

A minute later my husband asked, "What? Dry wheat toast and sliced tomatoes? No eggs?"

We both turned just in time to see Victor under the kitchen table, daintily finishing off a cheese omelet.

These dogs run us, all of us. We sit where they let us sit, and jump up when they command us to, and obey them when they demand us to pet them. They head butt our arms until we give in and stroke their heads and massage their backs, never mind that we were trying to read the paper.

So, as much of a workout that these dogs are, why is it we are absolutely wild about them? I think it's because Bubba and Victor think we are the most magnificent beings they have ever encountered. They leap to their feet whenever we enter a room, and when we come home from work they fall all over themselves in their excitement to see us. They stare at us, unblinking, as we sit by the fire and rub their fur. They truly cannot believe their good fortune, and they let us know that fact constantly.

Just now, Victor is stretched out on my lap and Bubba is asleep at my feet. For the moment, no one is demanding anything and the contentment I feel is immeasurable.

Really, I don't know what I would do without them.

A Sick Dog

I thought my dog was just tired at first. Resting after our long hike that lasted all afternoon. But then Bubba quit eating. And barely got up to greet my husband when he came home from work. The dog's eyes, usually warm and responsive, were dull.

All weekend we kept our eye on him, taking his food dish back to our bedroom where he lay pitifully, not moving his tail when we approached him. He was so sick he could barely look me in the eye. We debated taking him to the emergency animal clinic, but instead sat by him and rubbed his head. "You're okay, Bubba," my husband whispered.

We were all terrified he was not.

I took him to Dr. Keller first thing Monday morning for blood work and x-rays. Terrified of the vet as a rule, the dog panicked when they checked his temperature. Rectally.

Dr. Keller told me it was probably a tick-borne illness, but also said there was a small chance my dog had lymphoma. A teeny-tiny possibility. He held his thumb and forefinger an inch apart, and squinted through them, reiterating how infinitesimal this chance was.

One injection, four bottles of pills and three hundred dollars later, my dog bounded out of the car like he was an energetic puppy, and I cursed myself for overreacting. My children had been sicker than Bubba had been before I'd even given them Tylenol.

I was convinced it had only been a virus and that if I'd waited 12 more hours I'd be several hundred dollars richer, and my dog wouldn't have had a breakdown over the thermometer up his rear. Nonetheless, I gave Bubba his medicine diligently, surrounding every single pill with softened cheese or grilled salmon, disguising the tablets. He quickly wised up to my subversive technique. He carefully took the savory bites in his lips and clenched his teeth in a tight row as he swirled the tidbit around in his mouth before dropping the tiny pink tablet on the rug, where Victor tried to gulp it. I persevered, and was more disciplined about giving that dog his medicine that I ever was with my kids.

At the end of the two weeks of medication, my middle son kept the dogs while we went out of town. He took them down to his bachelor pad where they were hits with all five roommates, and the slew of constant visitors.

So when we picked the dogs up and noticed Bubba had relapsed, lying on his bed lethargically and barely eating, my husband joked the dog was merely hung over.

We watched him through another long weekend, covering him with a soft blanket as he shivered uncontrollable. The lymphoma was in the back of my mind as I rubbed my hand gently over his protruding ribs.

"We are not getting another dog," I remembered telling my husband firmly six years ago when the rangy hound mix showed up at the edge of our driveway. We already had a little dog and one pet was plenty for me. My family named him Bubba against my protests, and two days later we had him neutered. He's slept in our house every night since.

He loves us.

When my middle son came home from college after being gone for months, Bubba enveloped him and cried and cried, overwhelmed with emotion. Whenever any one of us has been down and out or broken-hearted, Bubba has known it, and stayed by our side, watching over us with warm, understanding eyes. His eyes are almond-shaped, and lined in black like Cleopatra's. They are kind, and expressive, and he speaks to us with them. When we are too-heavily-burdened, he is as devoted as any doting mother, following us to the bathroom, to the car, to bed, until we are ourselves again.

I couldn't let myself think about lymphoma.

We left the vet the second time with even more pills, and instructions to call if he didn't start eating soon. We all fretted over him, each whispering to him privately as we took turns sitting by his bed.

After three long days, Bubba got up out of his bed, slowly walked into the kitchen, and ate a few bites of gravy-coated meat. We were ecstatic. The next day he walked a loop around the lake. And the next day he ran toward my husband's truck as he pulled in the driveway, greeting his master.

"You're okay, boy. You're my best boy," my husband said as he rubbed the dog's silky ears. And Bubba looked at him devotedly, saying the exact same words to my husband.

My Dog Needs Braces

"I think Victor needs braces," I told my sister on the phone.

There was a heavy silence. Not even an exhale. I could hear her holding her breath on the line.

Victor is my little dog. My sister is not all that fond of dogs as a rule. I say that, but she's probably normal. She thinks they are actually animals, and should be treated as such. She has no problem making them stay outside, and wouldn't dream of letting them on the furniture. She thinks it's silly to dress them in clothes, or carry them around in a papoose meant for infants. Human infants.

No, she has no problem keeping all canines in their places, but especially my little Victor. She thinks I'm nuts. Whacko over my dogs. She has three grandchildren, two of them toddlers, and is over the moon over each one of them. She says that a couple of grandbabies would be a cure-all for me. She thinks I should buy a real live human baby a soft cotton nightie instead of buying a corduroy coat for my little dog. It was red.

I got my first little dog, Ruth Ann, when my oldest son turned 18. A little dog was all he wanted for his birthday. It was the last thing my husband wanted. In fact he forbade it, putting his foot down and throwing out ultimatums. When we returned from the Humane Society with a little black dachshund-min-pin mix, he melted immediately. And Ruth spent most of her time curled up on his lap. She fit into my shoe when we first brought her home, and chose my husband's fleece vest as her favorite spot. He zipped up his green fleece vest protectively, and I got used to the warm little bulge over his heart.

My sister rolled her eyes and flicked black dachshund hairs off my sweaters. She apologized to others about the state of my clothes. "Do you have any boundaries?" she asked.

My sister made no bones about it. She said we were certifiable.

But my sister, who thinks I am ridiculous about dogs, dropped everything the day Ruth Ann was hit by a car. She waited with us at the emergency animal hospital, her face pale and drawn. She offered us Coca Colas and sandwiches. She held my hand. And wrung her own.

A while after Ruth Ann died, my sister took me to the Humane Society. She knew we needed a new little dog, that a new dog would ease our heavy sadness. I didn't know it was so obvious.

The dog we have now, Victor, is the worst of all of them, according to my sister. She's never said so outright, but I can just tell by the way she makes me put him up in the laundry room whenever she brings the grandbabies over. She says it's because he snaps at them, and bares his teeth when they toddle toward him.

I tell her it's her fault. She chose him herself, handpicking him from all the dogs in the cages at the Humane Society. She pointed out to me how he tucked his little paws right under his chin, and curled into my arms like a newborn baby. He's the one. Look how he responds to you!

"Who told you Victor needs braces?" she asks accusingly on the phone finally. "Did your veterinarian tell you that? I don't think I've ever seen a dog with braces."

I can't stop laughing.

She doesn't think this story is all that funny. I wouldn't put it past you, she says. She twirls her finger by her ear as she speaks, indicating we are cuckoo.

But despite her own philosophy on dogs, I know where my sister's heart is.

Right by mine.

Always.

For the Sake of the Dogs

I'm a year shy of my 25th wedding anniversary. Twenty five years! A quarter century.

In a way, I feel like we've been together forever.

In another, I feel like we just got engaged.

We're at the mid-life crisis point, the place where people realize their mortality, and discontent and a slew of other things that make them buy fire engine red convertibles, and leave marriages.

I announced to my husband that divorce was not an option for him. I yelled it as loud as I could, actually, and we weren't even fighting.

We were walking around the pond together with our dogs, Bubba and Victor. My husband had to head back home early, and I was taking the dogs on another loop.

I started up the hill, calling the dogs to come with me. They both just stood at the edge of the lake, staring at me quizzically, then turning toward my husband. Clearly befuddled, neither animal moved an inch in either direction.

"Don't look back at them! Keep walking!" I shouted to my husband. "COMEBUBBACOME!" I bellowed, clapping my hands for emphasis.

The dogs grew more and more agitated, galloping five feet toward me, then five feet toward my husband. Their high-pitched, fretful yapping carried over the water.

"I'll just take them back with me," my husband yelled across the lake.

Their agitation quickly escalated into an all-out cacophony of anguish, and both the hound-mix and the Chihuahua-blend ran full throttle in one direction, then whipped around and ran the other way. They were obviously torn.

Irritated, I backtracked down to the lake and put them both on their leashes, muttering about their poor training and disobedience and high maintenance. I dragged them the direction I was walking, but they embedded their haunches on the road, straining against my pull.

"Oh, please!" I snapped. "This is ridiculous! You will see him in twenty minutes!" Distraught, they only yowled their pathetic, piercing cries.

"Hold up!" I yelled to my husband across the water. "This isn't working!" I unleashed the traumatized animals, and they took off full throttle toward him, screeched to a halt, then ran at mach speed back toward me, all the while moaning and whimpering and yelping.

To hear the two of them, you would think they'd been subjected to some form of medieval torture.

I could see my husband's neon green t-shirt as he approached the dam, and I threw up my arms in surrender.

"WE HAVE TO STAY MARRIED!" I shouted.

"What?" he yelled.

"Can you imagine the dogs if we were to get divorced?" I asked him as the dogs ran up to him triumphantly.

"The kids would be fine, but the dogs would be disasters," he said.

The dogs trotted along beside us, tossing their heads up as they looked up at us. Docile and subdued, they smiled their doggie smiles as they lumbered and prissed up the hill.

"I thought you wanted to go an extra loop," my husband said.

"No, I'll just come home with you."

"It's better if we stay together," he said.

"Yes," I answered, as I reached for his hand.

The truth is, I understand my dogs' reaction more than I let on.

The Empty Nest

It's been over a year since my last little chick flew the nest. All three of my boys have fluttered back for short little stints, landing for a random weekend during a holiday, or part of a summer. Then they're gone again, taking a chest of drawers or an ancient twin mattress or the coveted mini fridge.

It's what we want, right? Just like the mother bird pushing her fledglings out of the nest, we want them to learn to fly. That is the whole reason we taught them to use a can opener and put a paper towel over the Spaghettios when they cook them in the microwave. The whole point is for them to live on their own. To build their own nests, and flourish. Somewhat.

As a recent empty nester, I have discovered something very unflattering about myself. I want the best of both worlds where my adult sons are concerned. I want my boys to be financially independent, yet apparently I want them to be emotionally crippled. I want them, as full grown men, to sit anxiously by the phone in case I call and invite them to dinner at the last minute. Or on a picnic to the lake on a crisp autumn day. Isn't that what every mother wants deep down? Or that just the psychotic ones, of which I apparently am?

Luckily I have dogs I can attempt to screw up now that my sons have caller ID. The dogs actually embrace any of my attempts to hobble them emotionally. They don't mind being coddled whenever the whim strikes, or strapped to my side by a leash as I parade them around the neighborhood. Unlike my sons, who have moved on.

Recently dissed by all three of my sons over a lovely invitation to putter around in a boat at the lake (not actually skiing, mind you), my husband and I loaded up our two dogs who were actually ecstatic at the opportunity to get in the back of a hot car and ride up and down the hairpin curves to the lake.

Albeit uneasy over the long drive, the dogs ultimately couldn't believe their luck over scoring a day trip, even after we devoured our sandwiches right in front of them. I didn't want anyone getting carsick on the way home.

We rode slowly around the lake in a ski boat (think On Golden Pond with more profanity) as the dogs perched in the bow and sniffed the air. The little dog leapt up on the captain's chair with my husband, and the big dog lay across my lap as the sun dropped low in the October sky.

I caught my husband's eye and pointed at the dogs, each acclimated to their new surroundings on the water. We smiled at each other, smug with our bounty.

I think my husband and I both experienced a bit of a déjà vu as we watched a blue heron slowly flap its wings and glide across the cove. Wasn't it just the other day that our family weekend together at the lake was the highpoint of our boys' summer?

As I watch the bird, I can almost feel my middle son's hand on my chin, fragrant and sticky with syrup from the morning's pancakes, as he turns my face toward the water. Toward the heron.

"Wook, Mommy," he says, not yet pronouncing all of his letters.

My husband and I watch the heron move slowly over the water, almost suspended in the air as the bird beats his wings rhythmically. His little bird feet stretch out behind him over the water, so clear we can see every single toe.

And just like that, he is gone.

THE END

Thank you for reading Dogs and Love. I hope you remembered some of the dogs you have loved over the years as you read these stories. And maybe you are lucky enough to have your dog curled up in your lap, or snoozing at your feet as you read.

To me, dogs are old souls, and somehow meet our emotional needs on a deep level that passes understanding.

If you get a minute, I'd really appreciate it if you could leave an honest review on Amazon. Maybe say what you liked about the book, or didn't like.

I have a facebook page, https://www.facebook.com/DogsAndLove, where I collect interesting things about dogs if you want to check it out.

And my website is www.ferrisrobinson.com

Thanks so much for reading this book!

Made in the USA
Middletown, DE
01 August 2018